Foreword to the Second Edition

by The Right Honourable, The Lord Menuhin

This booklet is a valuable contribution to the preservation of instruments. It is invaluable to the player, to whom it cannot give satisfaction to handle a violin encrusted with rosin under the strings, with a dirty fingerboard and chin-rest and strings enveloped in resin and sweat. I cannot bear that kind of carelessness. I welcome this little book as I would a treatise on the teaching of violin playing.

An A to Z of Instrument Care
Second edition
(First edition ISBN: 0-9518823-2-5)

First published in the United Kingdom 1992 by Orpheus Publications Ltd, 7 St John's Road, Harrow, Middlesex HA1 2EE. Tel: +44 (0)181-863 2020.

ISBN: 1-900306-04-2

Printed by KSC Printers, Tunbridge Wells, UK.

Contents

Service Log

Date	*Repairs*

Instrument Details:

Instrument Repairers:

Notes:

Introduction

Car-owners, unless they are mechanics themselves, take their cars in for a service at regular intervals: motor tests make it obligatory. Instrumentalists should do the same. True, you don't put your life at risk if you have a badly serviced instrument, but you might jeopardise your livelihood. The best advice anyone can give on instrument care is to take your violin, viola, cello or bass once a year to a reputable luthier to be checked over. It may need little attention, but if it does, the trained eye will notice any small 'stitch-in-time' repairs that could save a great deal of money – and inconvenience – when they get serious.

Somehow, because there is a parenting element in one's relationship to a musical instrument – the caring way it is wrapped up and laid to rest in its case – owners are reluctant to hand over that responsibility to someone else. It is only when there is a serious illness, or an accident, that they call in the repair-doctor. So, what are the things professional players, students, teachers and amateurs can do themselves and when should they call in an expert? This comprehensive guide, arranged in A to Z form, tells you.

The book amalgamates advice generously given by several distinguished makers and players (see page 2). Though generally in agreement with each other, opinions occasionally diverged. All confirmed that 70 to 80 per cent of repairs could be avoided. What's more, they *want* them avoided – violin makers are not looking for repair work. At the same time, it cannot be emphasised enough that a precious instrument needs expert handling and there is no substitute for developing a good relationship with a repairer who will get to know you and your instrument. Even though occasional do-it-yourself techniques are given, don't do anything unless you are *100 per cent* confident in yourself.

The book starts with **A** for **Accidents** and works through to **W** for **Woodworm** and ends with **XYZ** for everything else.

Acknowledgements

My thanks to Charles Beare, Julian Boby, Arthur Burgan, Hamilton Caswell, Emanuel Hurwitz, Stephen Gottlieb, Dietrich Kessler, Yehudi Menuhin, Simon Morris, Guy Rabut, Marc Soubeyran, Peter Trevelyan, Adam Whone and Michael Yeats for their invaluable help with this book.

Accidents

Accidents do happen; the important thing is not to panic. Repair technology now is so good that almost anything can be done. Whether it is worth it or not, is another matter. But if the instrument is valuable, do go to a reputable repairer and don't pick someone out of the Yellow Pages. In some countries, Germany, for example, you can't become a repairer without a diploma, which guarantees a certain level of competence, but it is not, unfortunately, the case in Britain or the US.

Here are some precautions worth taking to minimise accident damage.

1. **If the fingerboard drops off**. Tune the instrument down a good fifth so you don't put pressure on the neck to warp, but make sure you keep the bridge in position, because the bridge also secures the soundpost.
2. **If there is a new crack or an old one reopens**. Don't touch it, keep it clean so that it can be glued together easily and invisibly. If the crack is near the bridge, loosen the strings.
3. **If the corners are knocked off**. Keep the bit in an envelope and carefully protect the raw edge so that it doesn't splinter, but not with fibred material that might catch in the wood. You can make a pad of strips of masking tape, pat it on your clothes to remove some of the stickiness, and put that over the raw edge. Some restorers will even recommend

Sellotape, but others winced at the vision of the damage this might do if the player then tried to remove the Sellotape as this cannot be done unless the right solvents are used. A golden rule is, ask your repairer what to do. If he, or she, is confident of getting the Sellotape off without harming the varnish, then use it, but never, *never* try to do it yourself. Have it repaired as soon as possible so that it can be fitted back easily.

4. **If the neck breaks**. There's nothing you can do – the instrument will almost certainly need a new neck grafted in.
5. **If the peg-box cracks**. It depends where. If in doubt, don't go on playing, it will just make it worse. Have it repaired straight away. However, it is possible not to notice a crack along the peg holes. If you find you are wanting to push the pegs in more than you used to, stop and look. Pushing in the peg is the worst thing you can do because it will make the crack worse.
6. **If the scroll breaks or chips**. This is mainly, but not entirely, an aesthetic problem. If you are abroad, and you can protect the raw edge, it can wait till you are back home. Keep the chip.
7. **If the bridge splits across the middle**. This will be a clean split along the annual rings. Sellotape (or similar) across the front and back will get you through a lesson, conceivably a concert. Some string teachers also carry little brush-jars of the fluid used to stick on false fingernails which would be effective in a crisis and on a strictly school instrument.

8. **If a string breaks**. Have a spare set, obviously! But if you do not have one and cannot borrow in an emergency, then try a reef knot, assuming of course that the knot is in the pegbox or below the bridge.

See also **Repairers** and **Restorers**.

Adjusters

See **Strings** and **Tailpiece**.

Adjustment

See **Set-up**.

Advice

Always take advice from someone you respect about which repairer to go to. Seek out other musicians if you are not in your own home town. Having found someone, trust their opinion in preference to that of your desk-partner or quartet colleague. Remember, that simple advice from a violin shop costs you nothing and can save heartache later. Most reputable repairers would rather give you a few minutes advice, say, on what kind of instrument you can or cannot take to Scandinavia or Malaysia, than pick up the pieces (literally) after you come back.

See also **Repairers** and **Restorers**.

Bow-bugs

Bow-bugs are to bow-hair as woodworm is to wood. They are tiny grubs that eat bow hair. If your hairs keep breaking, take a closer look. If the ends have been nibbled, then look at the bow – or more usually, the case – and see if you can spot a white grub, about 2mm long. If so, vacuum out the case, and you can get a treatment dust for the bow or a vapona to hang in the case. Ordinary clothes moths will sometimes get into a felt case, causing similar damage. Moth balls, or treated paper are the best protection for this. Bow-bugs are not, generally, a problem where the bow, or case containing it, is in constant use.

Bows

Use a soft cloth on the stick and frog every time you have stopped playing to prevent a build-up of rosin. It is unwise to take bows apart unnecessarily, because it is very easy to damage the bottom plate of the frog. Controversy rages about whether the musician should periodically wash the bow hairs in some sort of soap solution. This has been covered in some detail in

The Strad over the years. The repairers consulted felt that washing bow hairs is unwise because if some of the water gets into the mortices, it can damage the wood. On the other hand, the build-up of rosin, which oxidises and gets contaminated, can create a glass-like veneer on the hair which prevents the required grip on the strings. Just occasionally it can be worth washing a bow (children's are notoriously dirty in some cases). For this soda crystals or liquid detergent can be used and great caution is needed.

Bows are fragile, so it is best to avoid anything that would put stress on one part of the bow. This very easily creates a stress crack, which gradually becomes visible and it is here that it would break if put under too much strain. So tapping the bow on a music stand to clap the conductor may be courteous, but costly. Also, take care how you apply the rosin, because if you tend to put pressure in one place, this will cause stress. So will shaking the bow in the air to remove excess rosin.

When the head snaps, it is almost always because of a stress crack. It's obvious, but worth reiterating, never to put the bow on a chair or across a music stand – even those that have a bow-hanging hook at the back. More bow sticks get broken in this way than one could imagine. If the head does break off, it can be repaired and will play the same, but it can drastically reduce the value of the bow. To give some idea, a £3,000 bow with a broken tip can be repaired for perhaps £100. But after that it's only worth £300 – 500 even though modern mending techniques are so sophisticated that the playing qualities are not affected. A cheaper bow will be described as a 'write off'. It is worth remembering that insurance companies will ask for the pieces to be sent to them before refunding the full insured amount in the case of a write-off. You may prefer to ask for 90 per cent of the value if you keep the bits yourself. For very little outlay you can have the bow-head pinned or laminate-glued and keep a respectable spare.

If the wedge keeps coming out at the tip, it may be because it is too small or badly cut. This happens a lot on cheap children's bows and it can be pushed back in. If it happens on good bows, this may be a sign that it needs rehairing. In cheaper bows it may be the fault of a badly cut mortice. The wedge may also fall out if the ivory or bone face on the tip is cracked as it will not give the proper tension to the plug. Examine it to see if it needs replacing. There are three signs that a bow needs rehairing:

1. The hairs simply wear and break so you don't have enough of them to perform their function.
2. The hairs are wearing on one side more than the other. This must be watched as it will cause the stick to warp if not attended to.
3. The hair has stretched allowing the frog to travel too far (more than 4mm) from the leather lapping when the bow is tensioned. Never let this gap become so big that the thumb can sink into this to touch the stick, which would then become worn at this point, again seriously reducing the bow's value.

Rehairs are often done according to where the bow is to be most frequently used. Pit players at Covent Garden, for example, ask for a long rehair because the hair shrinks in the dry air of the auditorium. In New York the humidity in the summer and the dryness of the winters is an acute problem. Players undertaking a new contract can save themselves money by finding these things out before beginning.

When tightening the bow, stop before the gap between the mid-way point of the stick and the hair exceeds the thickness of the stick at that point (ie approximately a pencil's thickness). Some people don't tighten the bow enough at the frog and when playing the stick crunches against the strings. This damages or wears the stick especially if it is octagonally shaped. If you tighten it too much (as Kreisler did in the days when you could buy six bows at once and think nothing of it) you'll warp the stick and render it useless. (The story goes – very likely apocryphal – that Kreisler would walk back into Hills when he had got through his six bows and ask for the stick to be changed, keeping all the fittings.)

Take care of the thumb lapping at the frog because its purpose is to protect the bow (as well as give ease of handling). Make sure it is replaced before you get through to the wood. Keep octagonal sticks crisp at the edges: it devalues them if you let the corners get rounded. With a very valuable bow, it may be far-sighted to protect the maker's stamp from wearing out or getting dirty: get a bow repairer to fit a protective layer of clear plastic, or leather.

If the frog wobbles on the stick, it may be because the brass eye is too high, sticking out of the frog too far and touching the bottom of the frog mortice. Players have been known to give it a half-twist with the screw. DON'T do this; nine times out of ten it will damage the razor-sharp edge of the frog where it fits inside the facet on the bow stick. It needs to be done with fine pliers, preferably by an expert. A bow that wobbles at the frog will eventually warp the stick, making playing difficult and devaluing the bow.

Cellists, more than the other string players, have a tendency towards wearing the wood on the stick where it comes into contact with the hard edge of the thumb (sometimes the side of the nail). A remedy for this is to have a short rehair, but if the player needs a long rehair, a protective leather patch can be put in to protect the wood. It is worth remembering that one person would completely wear out the hand end of a bow in a lifetime's professional playing if no care were taken of it.

See also **Value and Restoration**.

Bridges

The bridge (together with the soundpost) affects the playability more than any other separate part. The quality of the bridge depends on its 'maille' a French word for which we do not have an exact equivalent. 'Grain' is the nearest, but it is not just the closeness of the annual rings that is important (ideally running straight across the bridge), but also the figure of the medullary rays (the flecks running down the bridge). The 'maille' is vital to the quality of the bridge as the sound travels down the rays to the resonating table beneath. Obviously the cut and fit is vital and, having found a good one, there's no reason why you shouldn't keep it a very long time. Some musicians change bridges like they change shirts; this is not necessary. Generally speaking, they have to be changed because they begin to warp, but a little attention can prevent this. There is a tendency for the bridge to bend forwards (towards the fingerboard) every time the instrument is tuned, or strings are changed (or backwards with cellos fitted with four adjusters). All the player need do is check its position from time to time and gently correct it. But not arbitrarily. The back of the bridge should be at right angles to the top of the instrument. If it isn't, put the violin on a cloth on the table, with the scroll furthest from you, and pinch the bridge with the two thumbs at the tail-piece end and very gently correct its position.

If it doesn't move easily you may have to loosen the strings slightly; in that case let the bridge lean backwards (towards the tail-piece) a little to compensate for tightening the strings again. To guard against the possibility of the bridge falling down when you do this (though it shouldn't), place a folded soft cloth under the tail-piece to prevent it clapping down on the table.

Another reason why the bridge might move is because the grooves are too small, or too rough or not lubricated enough. The strings pull it towards the fingerboard. Make sure the slots are all smooth and use a little dry kitchen soap, beeswax or graphite for lubric ation. (Note that graphite can make the bridge look dirty.) Bridge care is particularly vital if you have found the right one and want to keep it. However, if you do have to have a new one cut, always ask for the old one back so you have a spare for emergencies, and if the new one doesn't seem as good, you will have something to compare it to.

In extremes of climate, cellists and bassists may have to have two or three bridges to compensate for the movement of the wood between seasons. In winter, for example, the top dries out and contracts slightly so that the strings feel low. If this happens a lot, it is worth investing in a bridge jack, which holds the strings in position while you swap over bridges (rather like a tyre changing jack). If you have to change cello bridges without a jack, try to do it as carefully as possible so as not to disturb the soundpost. Always note the precise position of the bridge before removal. A tiny triangle painted in watercolour is easily removed and is better than anything that might harm the varnish though do be wary of water soluble varnishes.

See also **Accidents**, **Humidity, Strings** and **Set-up**.

Buzzes

A buzz is one of the hardest things to identify and it is difficult for a player to know when to call in an expert. The louder the buzz, the more the player tends to think it is because the bass-bar has become slightly loose, which is almost never the cause. It is probably best not to rush into curing a very subtle buzz immediately. It is always easier to track down a loud buzz than a soft one. Soft buzzes usually disappear or get louder and either way the situation is improved by leaving it for a while. A lack of humidity can cause repair-studs or linings to move very slightly and this in turn can cause small buzzes. Before taking any other action, leave the instrument in a more humid atmosphere to see if it makes any difference. Once you have decided the buzz *must* be attended to, there are some simple diagnostic tests that are worth trying.

1. Find out whether the buzz occurs on one string or on all four.
2. If it is on one string, is it all the way up the string or just on one note? If it is all the way up, then the chances are that the string might be winding loose on the core and the remedy is simply to get a new one. If the buzz is always on the open string, then it is probably a faulty top-nut groove and needs professional attention. If the buzz occurs in higher positions only, then it may be because the string is bumping into the grooves in the fingerboard. This may mean reshooting the fingerboard or setting a higher bridge. Only a professional restorer can judge.
3. If the buzz occurs on more than one string, you will need to look all round the instrument, and if it isn't caused by any of the more obvious things listed below, you'll need help. Even an expert can spend hours: one reported that a recalcitrant buzz turned out to be a tiny grain of sand lodged in the *f*-hole. So check:

   (a) **All the obvious rattling points**: string ends in

the peg-box; loose adjuster on the tail-piece; chin-rest against the tail-piece; the screw-legs of the chin-rest; the clearance of the tail-piece above the table (should be at least 1 mm); whether a sliding mute is rattling against the strings; and if the E-string bridge-protector is loose. Less obvious are: an ill-fitting soundpost; an ill-fitting bridge foot or if the last 2 – 3 cm of the fingerboard have come unglued at the base of the neck.

(b) **Purfling**. Strange as it may seem, the purfling is a frequent cause of buzzing – usually the loudest. Where the plates join the ribs, the purfling takes much of the vibration and can cause a weak spot that buzzes even when almost imperceptibly unglued. The commonest place for a buzz caused by loose purfling is on the bass side at the *C*-bouts. You can check this by knocking it with your knuckles: if you hear a solid sound of knuckle against wood, it is secure; if you hear a 'tzack tzack' sound or can feel a vibration in your thumb, then the purfling is loose.

(c) **All seams and the eight corners**. Once fittings are eliminated a buzz is nearly always caused by a loose seam at the back or front, or round the *C*-bouts. To see where it is, suspend the instrument by the neck and gently tap it with the knuckles all round. An open seam on the back generally creates a slight rattle if tapped at the top. Then look at all the edgings, carefully prising with your thumb to see if there are any cracks where the plates are glued to the ribs. A buzz can be caused by just a few millimetres' opening. If desperate – just before a concert, say – you can slip a tiny strip of paper to fit tightly into an open seam, but don't use any glue, or lose it into the interior, and only do it if the alternative is a noisy buzz in an exposed solo. Above all, don't try and glue an open seam yourself: quite apart from problems of using the right glue, few musicians have the correct clamps, or know how to use them. You can do a lot of damage by thinking you can just run a line of glue into an opening.

(d) **Cracks**. Look particularly at old repairs. Two thin cracks on the lower circles of the *f*-holes are particularly common; see if they move. If there is a crack anywhere, take the instrument straight in for repair before it gets worse. Remember that you can't see inside whereas an instrument maker can get a clearer picture. It is still wise to narrow down the possible cause before rushing to a repairer to have the top taken off and an experienced repairer would only take the instrument apart as a last resort.

(e) **The endpin**. All cellos and basses will buzz if the endpin is fully retracted, but if it buzzes in normal playing position, it could be because too much of the pin is still inside the instrument (have a few centimetres cut off), or it could be loose within the plug. A spiral of Sellotape round the pin can provide temporary relief. The violin saddle can sometimes work loose and cause a buzz (rare); make sure it is *very* firm in its socket.

(f) **The fingerboard**. A badly worn fingerboard with bumps and string grooves is a common cause of buzzing. It will need to be taken in for re-truing. Also check that the fingerboard is not becoming unglued from the neck – especially at the neck root.

(g) **Decorative fittings**. Gold-mounted collars on box-wood pegs sometimes come loose and cause buzzing. Decorative details such as mother-of-pearl inlay can also come loose.

(h) **Where the chin-rest meets the tail-piece**. Simply adjust the position of the chin-rest.

On viols, the strings can buzz on the frets if the fingerboard is not perfectly level (it is not convex as it is on violins). This can be compensated for to some extent by choosing appropriate fret-gut thicknesses, but it is a fussy procedure which is probably beyond most players and does not always fix the problem. It may be necessary to get the fingerboard trued.

Cases

Choosing the right case is crucial to instrument care. It also requires a number of other considerations that run counter to the safety of the instrument. The cases that give most protection are the most expensive and usually the heaviest; for cellists and bassists, especially young ones, this is a problem. Compromise must be reached, but it is as well to bear in mind what one is looking for in a case:

1. To hold the instrument securely with as little contact as possible with the case itself, especially round the bridge and scroll. Never put a smaller instrument in a case meant for a larger one unless it is firmly wedged with soft cushioning. Otherwise the bridge is in danger of hitting the top of the case and its feet could go through the table.
2. Violin and viola cases should support the neck near the root since this may prevent the neck breaking should the case be dropped. Often there's a little box here for mutes and rosin.
3. Cello cases should hold the cello in place at the endpin, where it is strongest and should secure the neck. The better ones have a slightly arched back so that you can't push the back in. The back shouldn't touch the cello, because an inadvertent knock will transmit straight to the soundpost and this could crack the plates – the worst place for any crack.
4. Check for a strong lid that will protect the bridge from any blows. Thin fibre-glass lids that 'ping' in and out when pressed are to be avoided.
5. Make sure all the fittings are properly secured and unlikely to fall off.
6. Think about weight and convenience. Do you want wheels fitted to pull along the larger strings? Or rucksack-style straps for carrying the smaller strings on your back? The more variables, the more

you will need to be alert to checking that their security is intact.

It is worth taking care of a case, just as you do the instrument, in order to get most wear out of it. The best people to repair and refurbish cases are good luggage shops or specialist case merchants. Cello cases, especially the fibre-glass ones, tend to warp slightly. You can prevent getting the fittings out of true by always doing up all the catches, even if the instrument is not inside the case. Indeed, it is good practice to make a habit of doing up catches at all times. Many an instrument has been damaged because its owner – or someone else – picked up an undone case leaving the unprotected instrument to tumble to the floor. Sometimes the fasteners on violin cases work loose: if in doubt, put a strap round the case.

Check, also, the fittings inside the case. Many bows have been damaged by inattention to their moorings, and bows that are loose in a case can fall on the instrument itself and damage the varnish. Look out for metal bow-clips inside cases and avoid them because they can damage the stick. They should have a Hill-type clip which is operated by twisting a knob and is much gentler on the bow. If you do have to make do with a metal spring clip, make sure it is kept covered with some soft fabric. Young players should remember to put violin bows away making sure that the hair is downwards when the bow is at the bottom of the lid and upwards when at the top so that any danger of getting the hair entangled with adjusters is minimised.

Handles and straps are particularly vulnerable and can be temporarily repaired quite easily. Worn lining fabric is also potentially damaging if it can chafe the instrument – in fact a great deal of unnecessary damage is caused by inadequately lined cases. Owners of the smaller strings do well to slip the whole instrument into a home-made silk bag. If you have a small-sized cello and a full-sized case, try padding out the bottom with a draught-snake (the sort usually placed at the bottom of a draughty door). Smaller cellos are often kept in padded cases because it is easier for young players to carry them around. Do remember to take the bow out of the pocket before removing the cover – many accidents happen to bows from this small inattention.

If you have an instrument, in its case, on the back seat of a car and cannot avoid contact with direct sunlight, then cover the case with a white reflective blanket, preferably microcellular or of duvet material, or with a silvered plastic sheet obtainable from outdoor and camping shops. This will save the dark cases from absorbing sunlight and roasting or blistering the instrument inside, which is a serious danger.

Finally, don't keep anything in the case that it was not designed to hold – not music, nor shoulder-rest nor sandwiches.

See also **Storage** and **Travel**.

Chin-rests

Early violins and violas, in the 16th century, had no chin-rests because technique was not so developed and players could support the instrument with the left hand. The need for stability and freedom in the left hand has led to the development of the modern chin-rest. It was probably initiated by Spohr who published his design for a 'violin holder' in 1832. There are now several different varieties, some of which can be harmful to the instrument. Obviously a first concern in finding the right chin-rest is comfort – and that depends on your own size and shape. The right chin-rest can solve all kinds of problems – backache, the sore patch on the neck ('violinist's rose'), bad posture, tense shifting and uneven vibrato.

In choosing, you should also be aware of the effect a new chin-rest may have on the instrument. Choose one that has as little metal as possible liable to come into contact with the wood (it should always be protected with cork or leather), and make sure you don't clamp it on too tightly as it may squash the ribs. You must also take care when loosening or tightening the chin-rest not to damage the varnish. Try to use the little keys that come with the rest, but if you lose this, then a paperclip will often do if used with caution.

Most chin-rests attach to the top and back across the ribs with tubular, threaded metal clamps covered in cork where there is contact with the wood. This cork will crumble over a period of time and must be replaced either with a similar thin cork or with thickish leather. The chin-rests that fit over the tail-piece are good for the instrument as they are clamped over the block, though there are players who say this spoils the sound and it can happen that this type of rest easily works itself loose so that one edge rests against the tail-piece, so damaging it slightly and causing a buzzing noise on some notes. There are padded chin-rests which cover all metal fittings with cloth – more expensive, but cheaper than the cost of damage.

A cloth over the chin-rest keeps moisture and grease from getting onto the instrument. Chamois is the best as it has a good grip and doesn't let moisture through. It also protects the player from the metal fittings and heat. In an extreme case of bulging ribs at the chin-rest, it may be advisable to have a thin plastic guard fitted here.

Cleaning

Everyone reading this will have made music with people whose violins are so caked with dirty rosin that they have the texture of hard ash. It doesn't take much imagination to see that this harms the instrument and its sound. A build-up of sticky deposits makes it hard to identify, let alone repair, cracks in the wood.

Start off on the right foot by having the instrument cleaned at its annual check-up. If it is a very valuable instrument, however, make sure that the luthier is sensitive to the authenticity and history of the instrument. Current thinking is that there is a difference between 'dirt' and 'patina' and some deposits are part of that instrument's past. An old instrument can lose value by being too zealously cleaned and brightened up. Avoid a build-up of rosin by dusting it off after each session. But if, in the rush of every day life, you forget, periodic cleaning with the right substance is a substitute. There isn't a lot to beat spit and polish (or a lightly damp rag) as much of the dirt is water soluble whereas varnish isn't usually. Do be wary, though, because there are some varnishes which are water soluble (certain Klotz models, for example).

Then there are fluids sold in violin shops (Vipol, Hills and others): some repairers suggest caution in using these as some of them contain turps as well as polish, which is not good for the varnish if overused. In fact, too much of this kind of polish will harden and be very difficult to remove. Look at the labels of any polish or cleaning fluid you buy, and make sure it contains no linseed oil – olive oil or almond oils are fine in moderation, but linseed should only be applied by experts.

If you do use such a fluid, the best way to apply it is as if polishing shoes. A tiny amount smeared on the corner of a dry soft cloth is all that is needed. Rub gently to dislodge the rosin or dirt and then buff it off with a dry part of the cloth. Never smear these polishes anywhere near an open crack as they will make gluing difficult when the crack is repaired. Also avoid getting it near the strings or bow because oily bow-hair on strings will result in slithery silence. Cleaning fluids don't, however, remove all the rosin and dry-wiping doesn't get rid of it all, however good you are about it. A valuable instrument needs professional cleaning every so often in ways that an amateur cannot do safely.

To clean the strings, try a good proprietary string cleaning fluid such as the one manufactured by Pirastro if the strings are caked with rosin mixed with sweat from the fingers. A slightly muffled sound is often a symptom of dirty strings and cleaning them revitalises the sound. The E-string may even rust (unless it is gold-plated or stainless steel) if a player has very sweaty hands. Yehudi Menuhin advocates pure alcohol or an eau de Cologne that is 90% alcohol (e.g. d'Orsay) or very fine metal wool. In both cases it is essential to put cardboard and soft tissue between the fingerboard and the varnished violin table so as to avoid any alcohol or metal wool coming into contact with the varnish. It is really best to avoid doing this unless you are 100% sure of yourself. Easier to take the strings off one at a time, clean them and put them back on – but not too often because the kinked peg-ends of the string often break through metal fatigue when put back into the peg-holes again.

If you should have a disaster and some solvent does run across the instrument, don't do *anything*; don't try to wipe it off as this will smear the fluid and make it much harder to touch up.

Some people confuse string cleaning materials with string oil. The oil is a vegetable product designed to nourish uncovered gut strings and prevent them getting brittle. It is not to be used on wound metal strings.

Cleaning inside the instrument should be done occasionally as dirt and dust balls gather. The traditional method is to pour a handful of fine lead shot through the *f*-holes, but lead-shot is not readily available and some care must be taken not to bowl the soundpost out of the way. Some people use rice, but restorers were chary about recommending this. If there is a reason for doing it yourself, make sure it is completely dry rice (warm it slightly in the oven first) because if it is even slightly soggy grains could stick to the interior. Drop in a small handful and gently sluice it round the interior, tipping to get into every corner. Then turn the instrument upside-down and carefully shake every rice grain out through the *f*-holes, taking the greatest care that it doesn't go flying out of your hands. A large ball of dust (known as the mouse) is collected by the dry rice and may have to be coaxed out with a pointed stick.

Rock salt is another amateur favourite, but it is not recommended. If any crystals get left inside the instrument they will attract moisture and could damage the linings. Violin repairers clean insides with a damp rag, but this is a risky exercise as in clumsy hands there is a danger of ripping the corner of the *f*-hole when trying to get the rag out.

Cleaning the fingerboard is too risky. It really needs alcohol to clean it effectively, but this can run into the varnish before you've noticed and cause permanent damage. You could protect the rest of the instrument with a sheet of cardboard (not a cloth) but don't take the risk with a valuable instrument. Run a silk rag under the strings every time you put it away to stop the finger-grease hardening.

One hesitates to mention this, but some amateurs seem to think you can clean an instrument with meths. Put it right out of sight and never, *ever*, think of it again.

See also **Bows** (for cleaning bow hairs) and **Value and Restoration**.

Cracks

See **Accidents, Bows, Buzzes, Cleaning and Value and Restoration**.

Endpin

Cello endpins can cause problems if they are not fully extended (see **Buzzes**). They can also cause a great deal of irritation if they don't screw up securely and if they don't rest firmly on the floor. There are a number of endpin holders on the market, each with its devotees. I haven't found one that is the answer to every type of floor surface, but it does help if the spike is sharp enough to grip. You can sharpen it yourself with a metal file – take the pin out of the instrument first. If it is very sharp, protect it with a rubber stopper (some stoppers grip very well on polished floors). A file is also useful for roughening up the end of the screw that holds the spike in position. If it is smooth, it does not grip the spike well. Take the screw right out and away from the cello to do this. Another temporary solution to sliding spikes is to rub the pin itself with rosin so that the screw has something rough and sticky to grip on. If the locking screw fails because the thread strips, several layers of Sellotape on the rod will stop it sliding in and will get you through a concert in an emergency.

And, obvious, but worth saying – always push the spike right in every time you lay the instrument on its side if taking a short break. If someone brushes by, the spike is a danger, not just to the person passing, but to the instrument. Of course, the endpin should always have a collar on it near the point so that it can't be pushed right into the cello. If this happens, it would go right through the ribs at the neck, resulting in expensive repairs.

Check that the wooden plug of your endpin is fully tight and snug in the body. The slightest looseness will cause the endpin to pull over at an angle and probably buzz. Either the hole in the body will need bushing or the endpin plug will need to be replaced.

Fingerboard

It will depend on the quality of the ebony – as well as playing style and frequency – how often the fingerboard needs truing. It can be anything from 10 months to 10 years. A fingerboard will need replaning and scraping (don't do it yourself):

1. If there are pits where the fingers hit the strings.
2. If there are tramline grooves where the strings have pressed into the wood.
3. If it is warped.

Players often do not notice these things. Warning signs are intonation problems or if the strings buzz on the fingerboard. If the fingerboard is very thin and weak, due to repeated retruing, it may need replacing entirely, involving a new top-nut and bridge as well. Fingerboards can become unglued from the neck. Obviously this will need attention, but if you can't get to a repairer in time, it's amazing how robust double-sided Sellotape can be for this.

See also **Buzzes** and **Cleaning**.

Fittings

See **Bridges, Chin-rests, Fingerboard, Nut, Pegs, Saddle, Shoulder Rests, Strings and Tail-piece**.

Humidity

Humidity is, possibly, your instrument's worst enemy. Ideal humidity is at least 55 per cent; anything below 50 per cent is dangerous. Once or twice a year in London, the humidity goes down to the high 20s, but in Canada and the Nordic countries, true of Finland too, it can get down to single figures.

Musical instruments do not respond well to lack of humidity, and dry heat is the worst (as in mid-West USA, the Middle East or the Nordic region). Homes or schools with central heating at full blast can be very harmful. The wood shrinks when it is dry and when it cannot shrink any further, it cracks. Part of instrument care is to protect it from the elements. Furthermore, insurance companies usually exclude cover for damage due to atmospheric conditions. A humidifier in the room where the instrument is kept is worth the cost, but is worthless unless you keep it topped up with water during dry spells.

For travelling about a Dampit humidifier is useful and it is better to over-use it than under-use it. It is, essentially, a long sponge inside a tube and held in the instrument through the *f*-hole. If you use one, you will probably have to soak it in water once a day during the summer, but a lot of damage is done by people who don't read the instructions that come with the humidifier properly and who put the sponge back dripping wet. If you are on tour, and low humidity is severe, leave the instrument with the case open in the bathroom overnight with water left in the bath. Another old-fashioned tip, that has some effect, is to keep a fairly fresh slice of potato in the case.

Another temperature hazard are the bright studio lights used in a recording session, which have been known to cause sudden, and alarming, audible splits in the wood. A humidifier is essential for studio work unless you are sure the environment is controlled.

There is very little you can do about damp heat, as in New York or Malaysia. You can get dehumidifying silica gel crystals (the sort that come in little packets with new cameras) which are effective if used in a decent quantity. A useful precaution is to have an arch protector made (it's not impossible to make one yourself but requires considerable skill). This is a wedge of folded cardboard, protected on its outside faces by a substance that will not damage the varnish (the insides of waxy milk cartons are ideal) which lodges under the fingerboard while the instrument is at rest and bound at the ends with Sellotape. It rests roughly half way between the end of the fingerboard and the neck, where the arching is highest and inhibits collapsing caused by high humidity. To be effective they have to be a perfectly snug fit – best to be aware of the existence of arch-protectors and get an expert to make one for you.

Winter cold is also guarded against by a humidifier which can relieve the 'tight' feeling that some musicians complain about. All you can do is temper the extremes and hope for the best. For example, if you take an instrument from the warmth of a house to a cold car, it is sensible to warm up the car first and not leave the case on the pavement while you brush the snow off.

Musicians who travel a great deal may have a dial hygrometer in the case to check on the air humidity. It is good practice to keep the instrument well-insulated – plenty of wrappings and a good case – because this slows down the effect of changes in temperature. Some cases claim to have an insulated shell.

See also **Cases and Value and Restoration**.

Insurance

You can get instruments included in a normal householders' policy, but most dealers recommend a specialist insurer. This isn't because dealers get a commission (though they do get a small one) but because, if something goes wrong, it is far better to be with a company that understands musicians and their problems. A specialist insurer has the benefit of experience in this one field. It is less likely to query accidental damage than a household insurer which has little opportunity for assessing instrument weaknesses. That said, do remember that insurance does not normally cover the player for damage caused by atmospheric conditions, such as cracks caused by excessive dryness. Also, you may not be covered for theft if the person to whom you have entrusted your instrument absconds with it.

Premiums are based on a percentage of value and generally speaking any instrument up to £5,000 value has a pre-calculated premium. Taking British Reserve figures for the smaller strings as representative, from £5,000 to £10,000 value is calculated at 0.625 per cent; over £10,000 at 0.469 per cent including unattended vehicle cover (there's a 20 per cent discount in Britain if you don't have this but many insurers in the US will not cover unattended automobiles at all). Bows, the larger strings and very valuable instruments are calculated on a different basis. Some instrument insurers will not penalise you with an excess clause (or deductable), ie deducting an initial sum when paying out a claim, though they usually do in the US on smaller claims. Percentage figures as given above are very similar but there are unlikely to be any discount premiums and there is normally a flat fee on lower-priced instruments. Clearly, it is advisable to have an up-to-date valuation, in case of disaster, and most restorers will include this in the annual check-up (yet another reason to do it). Keep a copy of the valuation (as well as an authentification certificate) outside the instrument case.

Insurance is a form of fail-safe. It isn't a substitute for care and attention to the instrument, nor do musicians treat it as such. An injured instrument can almost always be restored back to its original vibrancy, but sometimes – for reasons unknown – it loses some quality in its voice. No player willingly takes that risk with a valued friend.

There are other ways in which you can enhance insurance.

See **Loss or Theft**.

Loss or Theft

Have the instrument photographed from several angles and note down any special identifying characteristics, to be kept separately from the instrument. This will be useful for identification in case of theft (as well as for damage repair). Neighbourhood Watch schemes often have access to a property marker which you can borrow in order to give a code number only visible under ultra-violet light. This can be put in some discreet corner of the instrument and its case, and the code can be registered with the police. This fades with time, so don't just do this once and think you are safe. Renew it every five years. A more up-to-date system is to embed a tiny computer-recognisable chip somewhere, but this technology is far from widespread.

If the instrument came from a famous violin house, it may have a number discreetly stamped somewhere (Hills and Balmforths used to put a serial number at the end of the fingerboard on the G-string side: Withers used to have it inside the peg-box and Beare's and Paul Voigt put it above the endpin.) Make sure you are aware of any such number and keep a record of it.

Unique identification is more important than you might think. Police records are based largely on identity numbers or incontrovertible characteristics. You might think you'd know your instrument again anywhere, like a child – but the police won't think that's good enough. The way they deal with instruments reported missing is a caution in itself. You report it at the local police station. If – and only if – there is a unique identifier, news of its loss is circulated (loss or theft are initially treated the same). With 28,000 police officers in London alone, the chance of such a report being picked up is uneven, but if an instrument had been handed in to a different catchment area, the likelihood is that the two reports would match up. But if there's no label, no number, no special quirk, a lost and found report will remain opaque to the police computer system. In Britain, there is a National Identification Bureau at Scotland Yard which sets guidelines for what is regarded as identifiable: it wasn't drawn up by musicians.

There are various police books detailing property found in the streets, sometimes with pictures and description but you, the owner, are unlikely to see them. At one time all unclaimed items ended up with the Antiques Squad (disbanded some years ago but possibly to be reintroduced) and were eventually auctioned if not claimed. Apart from the police, there are commercial operations in Britain for tracing stolen items. One way is through *The Strad* and another is Smartaction in Glasgow. Similar organisations exist in the US and the American Federation of Violin and Bowmakers issues a regular listing of stolen instruments. An effective individual method is for the owner to circulate 100 or so copies of an information sheet to every violin shop in the country (or state).

If the fiddle is stolen, the situation is, curiously, not worse and could even be better. It isn't easy to sell valuable stolen instruments because violin shops are circulated with news of stolen property. The police, therefore, know who the likely offenders are. It may be only an impression, but it seems that matching known stolen goods with a loss report is easier.

As with everything else in this book, prevention is the best cure. You don't have control over absent-mindedness, foolishness or freak events, but you can put the instrument in the bank when you are away for any length of time. You can make sure the valuation is kept filed away separately from the instrument, so that a potential thief won't instantly recognise its value. You can keep a detailed and unique description of the instrument ready for circulation nationwide if the worst should occur. And trivial, but often forgotten, keep your name and address in the case so if it does get lost someone could return it to you.

Neck

Some makers, reputable ones, used to varnish the neck and occasionally this is thought to be protection from the acidity of the hands. However, it doesn't give a good surface for sliding the thumb and does not provide protection anyway. That is why your repairer may decline should you suggest doing this. It is better to get the neck periodically cleaned, oiled and polished. Depending on your personal acidity, this may need doing anything from every 6 months to 6 years.

See also **Accidents, Buzzes** and **Cases**.

Nut

Always lubricate the grooves of the top-nut with pencil lead when changing strings: the grooves should be rather less than a semi-circle deep. Misshapen or deep grooves can cause buzzes or can become so worn-down that the strings rest on the end of the fingerboard and buzz against it. A new nut is the remedy there.

Sometimes string groove spacing needs special adjustment for particularly thin or fat fingers.

Pegs

Ill-fitting pegs are a nightmare and generally don't succumb to amateur solutions. There isn't a half-way house between pegs that work and those that don't. The majority of peg problems require the holes to be re-reamed, or new pegs or re-shaping the old ones, and it is best to get an expert to attend to these. One way of diagnosing whether new pegs are needed is to measure the distance between the side of the peg-box and the peg collar. Ideally, it should be between 10 and 13mm for a violin, 20mm for a cello and violas depend on size. If the distance is considerably less than these, through constant pushing the peg home and wearing the peg-hole, then you are likely to need new pegs.

Stop-gap solutions like soap, chalk or graphite (any, or in combination) may give temporary relief, but they are not a cure. Chalk is an abrasive and will gradually make the holes bigger and the pegs smaller. The Hill peg compound (now available through violin shops) is universally recognised as an aid to making the peg grip in its hole, but some repairers feel it also has abrasive qualities and should only be used in moderation. Never be tempted to use rosin on a loose peg because it will become completely immovable. Check that the lips of the string-holes in the shanks are softened into a slight funnel-shape, because sharp corners to these lips will cut through the strings.

The best way of keeping the pegs and peg-box in good condition is to fit the strings properly so that there is no strain on them. They should be as parallel as possible in the peg-box; an angled string tends to pull the peg out of the peg-box.

See **Strings**.

Preventive Maintenance

Some random points:

1. Get an annual check-up – like going to the dentist.
2. Watch out for smoothness of cello edges; a tiny splinter will quickly get worse by snagging on the carpet.
3. Never, ever, leave a cello case with an instrument inside standing upright – students frequently do this, thinking, perhaps that it is smart, but if it is knocked over there can be hundreds of pounds worth of damage. Standard damage caused by knocking over an instrument in its case includes: broken neck, dislodged fingerboard, broken bridge, cracks in the ribs, seams coming unglued and soundpost cracks.
4. Don't leave an instrument, in or out of its case, in direct sun or next to a radiator, or in a car boot on a hot day. It could blister the varnish, cause cracks or loosen the glue that hold the instrument together.
5. Check the feet of shoulder rests to make sure the rubber protectors have not come off; the metal feet damage the varnish. Violin shops usually carry a range of spare rubber sleeves for the feet.

Protection from the Player

Heat from the hands and perspiration damage instruments. It's natural in energetic playing, so the more one can neutralise it the better. Some people have an acid sweat, some alkaline. Both damage the varnish over a period of time: you notice it only when the varnish begins to bloom, or go whitish. Precautions worth taking are:

1. Don't use handcreams before playing, especially not anything with lanolin in it. Ideally, wash your hands before playing any valuable instrument because this will get rid of the build-up of natural oils in the fingers.
2. Violinists and violists who sweat readily can protect the top shoulder – where the hand moves into the high positions and has most contact with the fiddle. A repairer can fit a strip of clear plastic film to the upper treble rib. In some rare cases plastic film may also be fitted to the rib below the chin-rest where overheating can occur. You would need to consult an expert repairer about this, as there can be a problem with fitting plastic to the shoulder of an instrument if moisture gets in and, in moving to the ledges of the plastic, causes the seams to open. An alternative is a layer of clear varnish which would have to be renewed at intervals.
3. Cellists and bassists or viol players can tie a small cape over the back of the instrument to protect it from body secretions. Jacket buttons are a hazard

for the unwary. Some dinner jackets are abrasive and will scratch the back of the instrument – not something high class tailors have considered, but worth a few minutes attention from regular orchestral players. It's easy enough to change to soft buttons.

4. The instrument should be at play or in the case and never anywhere else. A lot of players nurse the instrument while at rest, or talking during a break, thus gradually wearing the varnish. If it is always held by the neck and chin-rest and button, this damage is considerably diminished.

See also **Insurance**.

Repairers and Restorers

It ought to go without saying that you must go to a violin maker or repairer whom you trust, but it is worth stressing. Do recollect that anyone can call themselves a violin repairer, so your best bet is to make sure they have been accepted by their own community. There are charlatans in this business and you must be prepared to smoke them out. Rule number one is to make sure that the repairer or restorer you go to is affiliated to one of the reputable associations such as the International Society of Violin and Bow-Makers or local associations. The more expensive the instrument, the more vital this is. *The Strad Directory* and *Diary* are good sources of information on the relevant associations in each country.

See also **Value and Restoration**.

Ribs

Cellists and bassists have a nasty habit of sliding their instruments along the floor when laying them down or picking them up – just 10mm is enough to cause damage to the varnish. Over a period of time, the edges of the belly will splinter and gradually the edges will be worn down to the ribs (especially on the treble side). An experienced luthier can correct this and some advocate giving a little extra strengthening here to school instruments as this kind of damage is extremely hard to prevent.

Rosin

See **Bows** and **Cleaning**.

Saddle

Check that the ebony saddle (or bottom nut) has not become unglued and loose, or that it is not too long, which would have caused little splits in the table at either end of the saddle. A split on the right side of the saddle is in a direct grain line to the soundpost and there could be a danger of it splitting right up if the instrument is inadvertently knocked at the end when it is already weak there. If the saddle is loose, the sound suffers.

Schools

Few music schools have a policy of teaching students how to look after their instruments. The Junior Department at the Guildhall School of Music and Drama runs annual instrument care workshops and issues new students with a list of Dos and Don'ts, the Royal College of Music has a short-list (very short) of guidelines for students borrowing from its collection and the Royal Academy of Music also offers tips on instrument care. Similarly the Juilliard School has regular annual lectures on instrument care, but few other institutions make a point of this. Perhaps more should. In ordinary schools the shortage of teaching time is frequently so acute that teachers have enough to do to impart the basics of instrumental playing. Nevertheless, good habits are formed early and it should be possible to introduce basic care into the routine.

Scroll

See **Accidents**.

Seams

A commonly necessary repair is to seams that come open. As a player, you may not notice this unless the instrument starts to buzz and that leads you to the checking routine given in **Buzzes**. It is wise to cast your eye round the seams from time to time and make sure they are firmly glued. Otherwise you could find yourself applying polish, which then gets into the seam, thus making it very difficult for the repairer to reglue (and expensive for you).

Set-up

An instrument purchased from a reputable shop should be well set-up when you buy it. If you acquire an instrument from a private source, adjusting the set-up is an obvious first step – particularly the height and angle of the bridge, the position of the soundpost, the movement of the pegs and the suitability of the strings. Thereafter, players often forget about these things until something goes wrong, but you should keep an eye on the set-up even though it is something that will be automatically checked in your annual check-up and any adjustments made. After all an instrument is unlikely to stay in adjustment all the time: it changes with the change in the seasons, or with different climates when travelling. The chances are that you will need different bridges for different parts of the world. All set-ups have to be local, so when you travel you might need to seek out a local restorer who can make the necessarily adjustments. Caution is advised: a soundpost could be further from the bridge when the instrument is dry and stiff (say in California), but that wouldn't then work in London and New York. So deciding whether or not to have the set-up altered is something of a nightmare for touring musicians.

Some people alter the set-up in paranoid fashion with alarming frequency. This doesn't enhance the instrument which will suffer from too many shifts of position of the soundpost, especially if you go for a tighter fit than the instrument can take in the search for brilliance of sound.

Baroque set-up is a specialist area and the whole issue of string sizes and maintenance is different for different periods so go to someone who has expertise in Baroque instruments.

See **Bridges, Pegs, Soundpost and Strings.**

Shoulders

The hand has more contact on the shoulder in the higher positions than anywhere else on the fiddle and it may need revarnishing or protecting with thin, clear plastic. This is important because if the varnish wears down to the wood through constant touching and moving through high positions, the perspiration gets through the raw wood and can dissolve the glue inside, loosening the linings.

See **Protection from the Player**.

Shoulder Rests

Shoulder rests, arguably, can have more effect on the player's own health than any other accessory. But backache, muscle tension and related disorders are not the subject of this book. At the same time, it is worth considering that while a shoulder rest is enhancing, or damaging, your own comfort, it could also be harming your violin or viola. Shoulder rests, because they are put on and taken off every time the player plays, must be constantly checked for smooth edges. The rubber or leather feet, which touch the wood, fall off quite easily or else the rubber hardens. They'll need replacing at least every two years. Restorers commonly see four grooves worn into the edge of violins from shoulder rest damage. Don't keep putting off replacing them: get a supply of spares so that nothing hard will chafe the edges of the violin as you play.

Soundpost

Like the bridge, this is a small but crucial part of the instrument, and not to be tampered with unless you know exactly what you are doing – it's all too easy to cause damage that you cannot actually see. It's just a plain stick of straight-grained spruce, but the correct size and position have a major effect on sound.

On the whole, once the soundpost is adjusted to your satisfaction, you need not pay it much attention. The exceptions are:

1. **If it is a new instrument**. The belly wood may not have settled and it may need a new, longer sound-post. If the instrument has lost some of its sparkle or zest, it could be that.
2. **If the soundpost falls down.** Clearly you can't go on playing; but also, make sure there's no danger of losing it through wide *f*-holes, or worse. If there is, fish it out and keep it safe; if not, leave it where it is. Let the strings down immediately, but only by three or four semitones so that the bridge remains in position.
3. **Lack of balance**. Occasionally the tone becomes unbalanced and you may wish your luthier to reposition the soundpost. It is best to be present to have an interactive playing and checking session.

Storage

Storing cellos and double basses in schools, colleges or rehearsal rooms can invite damage. It is clearly best if there is space round the walls so that each instrument has its own parking position with wooden guides at right angles to the wall to hold the neck and a strap to secure it. Failing that, they are best stored on their sides, parallel to one another. Or if not in use, then they can be stacked in a corner with the strings inwards, the endpin being kept sharp enough to prevent the instrument from slipping.

Violins and violas require shelf space. They must, naturally, be stored away from direct sources of heat.

See also **Cases**.

Strings

Choosing the right strings is not part of instrument care, though it is worth checking what tensions are best for the body. The choice of strings is sometimes said to be the third element in the combination of person and instrument: it is a highly individual matter. Most people know that strings must be changed one at a time. Few realise the importance of keeping them as parallel as possible in the peg-box; an angled string tends to pull the peg out of the peg-box. If you can follow the Beare or Voigt method, so much the better. (See the diagrams on following page.)

Use a little graphite (or pencil-lead) or a dried sliver of bathroom soap on the bridge grooves and top-nut whenever you change strings. This ensures that the strings run smoothly in their grooves and don't break because of too much tension or pull the bridge towards the fingerboard and warp it. If your strings almost always snap between the nut and the peg box, it is either because the grooves need lubricating, causing that part to be too tight, or they may be snagging on another peg (caused by wrongly positioned holes). If

Beare Method

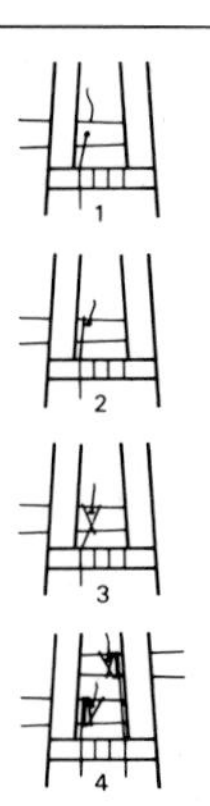

1. Put string end in through hole in peg, leaving a small amount protruding.
2. Wind first turn with string on peg-handle side of loose end.
3. Wind second turn on other side of loose end.
4. Wind remaining turn(s) on peg-handle side again, moving outwards to check.

Voigt Method

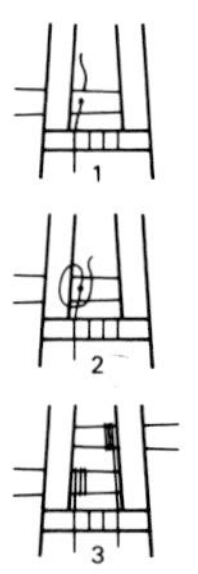

1. Put string end through hole in peg.
2. Pass string end underneath string from outside.
3. Wind up and guide the string on to the side of the peg-box.
4. Make sure that the string is on the side (G and D on the left, A and E on the right). Don't have too much string round the peg.

If the above instructions are followed it will not be necessary to push the peg in, and therefore avoid breakage to the peg box and scroll.

they snap between the bridge and tail-piece, it is because the bridge grooves need lubricating or smoothing. Attend to it as you change strings.

There is some disagreement among restorers about whether the string should touch the peg-box cheeks on the peg-head side of the peg-box. Reasons for this are that it helps to keep the strings parallel and that a little pressure against the peg-box helps the peg to stay in place. The reasons against are that it may damage the string and cause it to break, and if there is no gap, further winding will jam in between the already wound string and peg-box side. This will result in screwing the peg further into the peg-box causing it to become hard, even impossible, to turn. Such wedging can often be a major cause of peg-box cracks. A useful compromise is to have the string close to the peg-box wall (head side) but not actually touching it.

Two small tips for string-care:

1. Glue (or have glued) a little saddle of vellum on the top string groove of the bridge. You can then dispense with the plastic sleeve that comes with the string to prevent it cutting into the bridge. (Some violinists feel this makes a difference to the quality of the E-string.)
2. If you get broken loops on the E-string adjuster, you can now buy packets of plastic saddles to fit into the adjuster hook and protect the loop. (They are manufactured by Pirastro.)

So obvious as to be barely worth mentioning is the precaution of carrying one (or two) spare sets of strings. One set might be a perlon-centred string because they don't stretch and can be used immediately.

See also **Cleaning** (strings), **Buzzes** and **Wolf-notes**.

Tail-piece

Check the tail-gut, or tailon, periodically. Real gut tends to fray. It has been known for it to snap in the middle of playing, with disastrous consequences that can be imagined. In fact, few players of modern instruments now use real gut, so the chances of this happening have been minimised. Baroque instrumentalists, of course, do prefer a gut tailon (as they do strings) and are in the habit of looking after it. Whether a modern or Baroque player, it is worth carrying a spare tailon for emergencies. They are not difficult to fit, but the adjustment and trimming should be done by a violin restorer as soon as possible.

All tail-gut stretches over time and this is one of the things a restorer will look at when doing an annual service. A rough guide is to see if the free string length between the tail-piece bar and the top of the bridge is about one sixth of the distance between the bridge and the nut. In full-size violins this should be 55 – 57mm. Generally, where the set-up is correct, plucking the G-string behind the bridge will sound a D; the D, an A, and so on. However, there are sometimes very good reasons why the distances may vary from the textbook solution – to avoid a wolf-note, for instance.

Then check the adjusters, making sure they don't scratch the table. It's worth periodically unwinding them so that the lug comes back up to the top and then tune from the peg. Some adjusters have rough edges at the point where the string hooks over. Make sure this is smooth; if not, a needle file is all you need. Avoid using four adjusters as this puts extra weight behind the bridge. If it is necessary to do this (for children's instruments) then try to get a tail-piece with inbuilt adjusters as these are lighter and work better.

Double basses, because of their size, do not use ordinary tail-gut, but copper wire or galvanised cable. Metal fatigue can set in, which is one reason why tuning basses to a higher pitch than normal can cause extra strain.

Theft

See **Loss or Theft**.

Travel

Apart from worries about changes in temperature (see **Humidity**), this is more of a problem for the larger fiddles. The dilemma is whether to buy an air-ticket for your cello or bass and have it sitting next to you, or whether to put it in the hold. If you have an Amati double bass (as Gary Karr does), there's no question of treating in any way other than as a treasured relative. There is a new generation of flight cases, some even containing inflatable air-bags between the instrument and the shell. If the instrument is not valuable, you could try having a crate built round it. Some people recommend taking the bridge, tail-piece and soundpost out and having it re-set-up at the destination. This seems extreme, but it will at least protect the danger areas. If the instrument does have to go into the hold, it's worth trailing after it and making a nuisance of yourself so the handlers know how fragile it is. As for trains and buses, the luggage rack is not a good place to put an instrument. Apart from the danger of heavy suitcases falling on top of them it is surprising how many instrumentalists (young and old) have forgotten them there.

The string action (clearance between the strings and the fingerboard) increases in damp climates and decreases in dry conditions. Travelling cellists and bassists sometimes have two, or even three, bridges of various heights and some double basses can be fitted with screw adjusters in the legs to vary the height.

If you can afford a second, perhaps modern, instrument for travelling, some travel anxieties can be lessened. The more robust an instrument, and the fewer repairs it has had in its lifetime, the less at risk it is from travel and changes in climate.

Tuning Problems

Some players blame 'false strings', but this is very rarely justified as strings are made to high standards. If an instrument suddenly seems hard to tune (tested by playing perfect fourths across the strings at the harmonic at the centre of the string), there can be a number of causes:

1. The bridge or nut grooves are too small, or too rough or not lubricated enough and the strings are not sliding properly. Make sure the slots are all smooth and use a little dry kitchen soap for lubrication.
2. The fingerboard is out of true (see **Fingerboard**).
3. The ebony saddle (or bottom nut) has become unglued and loose (see **Saddle**).
4. There is a crack or open seam somewhere (see **Buzzes** for ways of identifying cracks).
5. The tailgut is stretching (see **Tail-piece**).
6. The pegs do not fit (see **Pegs**).
7. The soundpost has shifted from its optimum position (see **Soundpost**).
8. The player is having a bad day!

Value and Restoration

A valuable old instrument deserves special care – as does any fiddle with a good sound. Monetary value, however, is an issue, especially where people have mortgaged their houses to buy a Golden Period Strad. With a priceless instrument or bow, it is foolish to indulge in any of the stop-gap solutions offered in this book. Even cleaning is best left to experts. Purity achieves the highest prices and it is unwise to clean even a dark sticky accumulation of rosin if it has been there for a couple of hundred years. Who knows what lies underneath. It is best to be cautious and steer clear of any restorers who offer to do too much cleaning or retouching or restoration. Entrust it to a restorer who will do whatever is essential, but leave no visible trace of what he or she has done.

However, there are no rules in this game. If you acquire a badly damaged instrument – or yours suffers a near-fatal accident – the dilemma about how much repair to put into it is acute. There is a real worry that, however sensitive the repair, it may lose the special magic that gave it its value. But conversely, an instrument of excellent pedigree that just failed to attain the first rank in the eyes of the world – if reassembly becomes necessary – may take on new life blood it never had before.

Most small cracks – if caught fresh – can be repaired invisibly and should not affect the value of the instrument at all. New necks don't affect the value because most old instruments have had to have a new neck grafted at some time during their lives. And, of course, bass bars are renewed periodically as well. The damage that does drain £1,000s away includes:

(a) any marks on a virgin instrument;

(b) bad repairs;
(c) if an important part is not original;
(d) stripping it down and revarnishing.

See also **Insurance** and **Repairers and Restorers.**

Varnish

Varnish is not just a matter of aesthetics: it protects the wood. But with particularly old or precious instruments, restorers and players are reluctant to tamper with the natural wear and patina by retouching the varnish. There is much controversy in the trade about when it is appropriate to repair the varnish. As far as the player is concerned, the points to worry about the varnish are:

1. If there is a scratch or chip which spoils the look of the instrument, it should be repaired and the varnish blended in. This can be a larger problem than might appear as the scratched surface is not level with the rest of the instrument and building it up, while blending the colours is an art.
2. If the ground wears away and exposes the wood itself, then the varnish may need retouching. Many connoisseurs believe that players shouldn't worry if the coloured surface wears away because it is the underlying ground that is important. On old instruments, the varnish has often worn in places to expose the ground. But if it wears down to the bare

wood, then the wood becomes like blotting paper and will absorb dirt and moisture. Then it will become permanently discoloured.

3. On a new instrument, players seem to think it necessary to keep the varnish looking pristine and constantly ask for a retouch. In fact, the gentle wearing of the top varnish does no harm and is part of the natural wear and tear that gives an instrument its individuality.

Never, ever, be tempted to do a 'Do-It-Yourself' retouching job on the varnish. Good varnish retouching is such a difficult and sensitive art that many restorers think it to be the most challenging branch of the trade. Blending invisibly with an old varnish is much harder than revarnished from scratch. Only ever entrust retouching to a seasoned expert.

Sometimes, the varnish, which protects the instrument, needs protecting itself by fitting a plastic shield to the shoulders.

See **Protection from the Player**.

Wolf-notes

Every instrument has a wolf-note: whether you can hear it or not is another matter. Look for it on a violin at B flat to C, on a viola at E to F sharp, and on a cello at E to F sharp. Basses depend on size. Wolf-notes are caused by excess tension or by a break-down in acceptable pattern of vibration. A repairer will try the following:

1. Check that no part of the instrument has become unglued (see **Buzzes**).
2. Change the string to a thinner one with less inertia.
3. Alter the sympathetic vibration of the strings, possibly by lengthening the tail-gut to give a slightly shorter overall string length.
4. Adjust the bridge or soundpost or fit a heavier tail-piece.
5. Fit a wolf-note eliminator to the string, behind the bridge. When moving the eliminator (a small brass tube) nearer or further from the bridge, the wolf-note can be effectively altered in pitch and placed on a quarter tone or a less vital note. It will also reduce the wolfing to some degree. The third string is a potent wolfer on the cello: if the suppressor doesn't make any difference, the chances are you haven't tightened it enough. Remember to check the rubber feet from time to time to make sure they have not hardened and are not harming the wood.
6. Fit an internal eliminator (the wolf resonator) which absorbs the wolfing note. As yet these are only made for cellos and are very effective.
7. Reduce downward pressure by lowering the bridge.

Only items 1 and 2 can be done by the player and are subject to trial and error. In fact, the whole subject of wolf-notes is a quagmire of possibilities and requires further research.

Woodworm

It is rare to come across live woodworm in an instrument that is being constantly played. Whether the constant vibrations prevent the grubs settling is a curious question. If you acquire an instrument with tiny woodworm holes, you may be able to see whether or not the worm is alive by whether fine white dust settles around the holes. On the whole, though, only the exit holes are visible and by that time the worm could have been long gone. The instrument may need professional fumigation. You won't do any harm, however, if you squirt a few drops of worm-killer through the *f*-holes in the direction of the infestation to deal, internally, with any further woodworms that might not yet have exited through the exterior surface. A *few* drops.

By the time the holes appear, the damage is already done, and you can't ever be sure how much the wood has been weakened. What you should avoid, though, is pressing in the cardboard – thin ribs of a wormed instrument and so increasing the damage. Restorers can get some idea of the hidden extent of the worm damage by looking inside through the bottom hole while shining a strong external light on the body. If the wood is not weakened, the restorer will leave it. If it is – and the instrument is worth the time and trouble – the wood can be strengthened both structurally and cosmetically. However, if you do acquire an instrument from a distinguished violin house which has visible signs of woodworm, you can be sure of one thing – it will have been appropriately treated.

Further prevention is assisted by ensuring that your home has a current woodworm treatment certificate throughout. Spray a tiny amount of woodworm fluid onto the lining of your case; the smell will repel future woodworm beetles. Storing the instrument by wrapping it in newsprint is also supposed to deter infestation.

XYZ

No doubt there are a myriad of miscellaneous matters of instrument care not touched upon in this book. The advice is the same as it has been throughout. If the instrument is precious, take it for a service about once a year and only entrust it to a trustworthy repairer. If the instrument is not valuable but nevertheless plays well, you can make a few adjustments yourself – always bearing in mind the advice of the restorers given in this book. If the instrument is not valuable and does not play well, but it is all that can be afforded at the time, it is still worth giving it care and attention. Minor adjustments could improve its playability. It is, after all, rare that a musical instrument, unlike a car that constantly fails its motor test, ends its life in the scrap-yard.